GHOST MACHINES

BEN MIROV

Design by M Kitchell

Library of Congress Cataloging-in-Publication Data

Names: Mirov, Ben.
Title: Ghost machines / Ben Mirov.
Description: Greenfield, MA : Slope Editions, 2016.
Identifiers: LCCN 2015039683 | ISBN 9780988522145 (pbk.)
Classification: LCC PS3613.I765 A6 2016 | DDC 811/.6--dc23
LC record available at http://lccn.loc.gov/2015039683

INTRODUCTION
DOUGLAS KEARNEY

Reading *ghost machines*, I am reminded of Brian Eno and David Byrne's *My Life in the Bush of Ghosts*, J Dilla's *Donuts*, or DJ Shadow's *Endtroducing....* In these sonic works, archives reanimate into loop driven compositions that stave off endings. Refrain riddles these poems, deepening echoes that re-orient and destabilize. "A frozen lung tree"—a persistently repeated phrase, is an anatomical metaphor, an abstracted image of networks, part of a grotesque arbor—but in all cases, unable to provide air, for us every tree's most vital fruit.

Yet, these poems refuse stasis, gently accumulating new possibilities.

Possibilities for what? A kind of existence in (spite of) the code(s). If there's such a thing as "Ghost Mode," then one can move in and out of it, just as these poems shape shift, coalescing into a language via crosshatches of signal and noise, neologism and homophonic pun. Just as these poems move be-tween letter, glyph, and emojis for feelings we have yet to catalogue. Just as these poems imagine teem-ing voids and wet light—birth into a late night game of Space Invaders.

There is a game here. A game with narrative (this collection is part speculative fiction). A game played with "the dead part in everything." The part that lives, I think, as a ghost, when the rest of us dies. Is that another word for posterity? The repetitions shuffle in interval, adding new fragments from Rilke, Borges, and a video gaming manual. I can read the idea of a "ghost machine" as part of a factory that produces specters. The "echomorphs" section—whose poems assume flickering typographic contours—brings to my mind "ectomorph" a litheness that slides into "ectoplasm"—haint lubricant. Echo itself is a ghost of utterance, the repetition Mirov employs so diligently, so searchingly haunts the pages. As I read and reread, dogging the lines and their changes, I realize that refrains look backward as they move for-ward, like people running while glancing over their shoulders. Then I am the ghost, chasing the language, not letting the language be.

What didn't we leave alone that led to the ill weather that is this collection's landscape? Perhaps the Industrial Revolution gave us the inkling of the mechanic as a synonym for "the future." Science Fiction has codified this relationship. And even so, we can see many people in the U.S. have become casual cy-borgs, our smartphones acting as Tony Stark-like exoskeletons for our brains, our eyes and ears. And this makes it possible to read ghost machines as an ending. The trace of human apocalypse and ma-chines—Asimov's *I, Robot*, *The Terminator* and *The Matrix* franchises, *A.I.*, Dick's *Do Androids Dream of Electric Sheep*—are certainly part of the pop-cultural code of mecha-anxiety. But a ghost machine may be a machine that dies, muttering in its brittle housing lines like: "Dear Hibernation: / motes of dark are functioning / capsules of the night..." and "a tune of non-being / += ⸎ing the void / and sound ma-chine..." and "asstralylogism/ bemesticatorialloodge / ismaticsologismahybrodomina...."

Finally, a book of poems is itself a ghost machine. Pages, after all, are white sheets adjusted for us to see through. This book, it seems to me, is about what's left. What remains—ice, night, and strange ech-oes. *ghost machines* stays with me that way, lingering every time I set the manuscript down. Called me back to its shadows of shadows in ways I've rarely experienced taking my turns here, in the normal world. It's your turn, now.

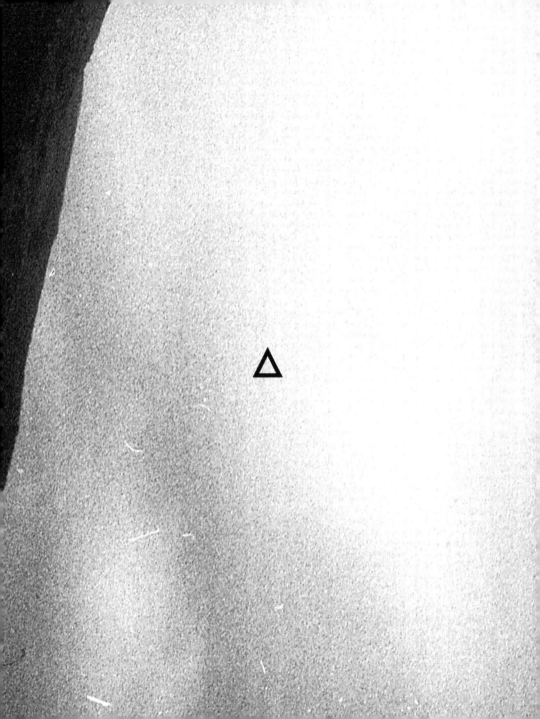

(...)

darklings

(...)

arklings

(...)

echomorphs

(...)

(d)rifters

(...)

knife/forms

(...)

sound shakes
a little
    underwater

in the
domain of
eternal night

a frozen

lung

tree

fading in
the dark

pulses its
    swimming bells

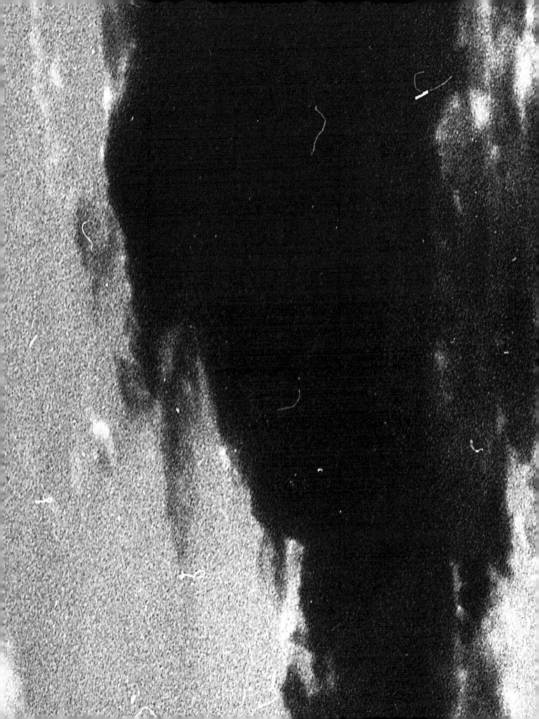

Ghost mode takes you to a different reality—a plane parallel to the normal game world where the current mission takes place. Ghost mode is only available in multiplayer games, and only to human players (AI-controlled players cannot switch to ghost mode). While in ghost mode, you still take certain actions—while other human players take turns in the normal world. (i)

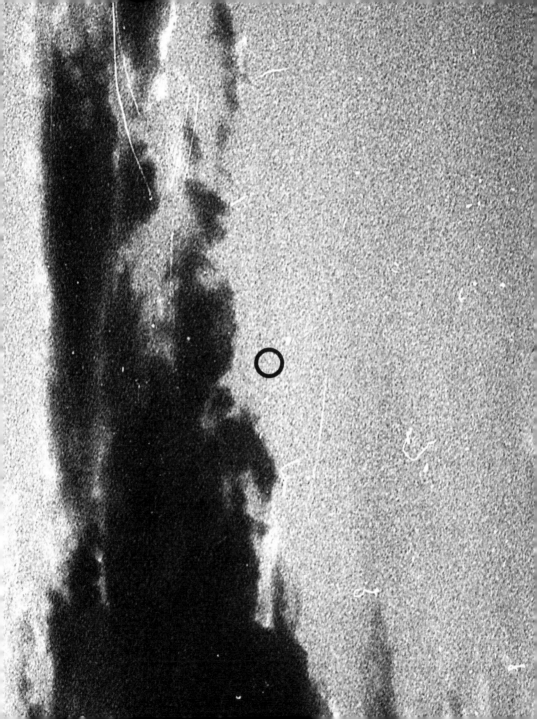

the sound of static

floating in the dark

where shadows make shadows

floating in the dark

nothing solid clone

piecing shit together with its sound

the fingers and the teeth

floating in the dark

shaped like sleep

wet with dew

nothing solid clone
floating like music
the sound of music
fading in the dark
the dead part in everything
shining and dull
its hands are raised
like it's begging for food
the fingers and the teeth
fading in the dark

nothing solid clone
pulses its swimming bells
a frozen lung tree
fading in the dark
the sound of static
music in the dark
the nails and the teeth
the shadows and the teeth
nothing solid clone
shaped like sleep

echoes pierce the light

shadows and ice

filling the void

preparing for an entrance

nothing solid clone

pulses its swimming bells

where shadows make shadows

floating like music

fading in the dark

echoes pierce the light

the dead part in sound machine

shining and dull

its hands are raised

like it's begging for food

motes of dark are functioning

the shadows and the teeth

the nails and the teeth

filling the void

a frozen lung tree

wet with dew

nothing solid clone
floating like static
fading in the dark
the nails and the teeth
the dead part in everything
shining and dull
its hands are raised
like it's begging for food
the shadows and the teeth
preparing for an entrance

nodding dead in silence
nothing solid clone
piecing shit together with its sound
the fingers and the teeth
life shakes underwater
shaped like sleep
wet with dew
preparing for an entrance
all flash no substance
filling the void

shaped like sleep

the shadows and the teeth

floating in the dark

piecing shit together with its sound

nodding dead in silence

nothing solid clone

where shadows make shadows

shaped like sleep

the sound of static

shaped like sleep

preparing for an entrance
the fingers and the teeth
fading in the dark
where shadows make shadows
fading in the dark
nothing solid clone
preparing for an entrance
all flash no substance
shaped like sleep
wet with dew

a frozen lung tree
pulses its swimming bells
floating in the dark
shining and dull
figment in the dark
its hands are raised
like it's begging for food
the fingers and the teeth
where shadows make shadows
shaped like sleep

Since my early years until now, the natural world and its visual wonders and horrors—man-made devices with their mind-boggling engineering feats and destructive abominations, elusive human nature and its multiple ramifications from the sublime to unbelievable abhorrences—to me are all one. It is in the spirit of this feeling that the ghost machines have occurred. As for my contemporaries, it was my personal friends who were the other basic influence on the ghost machines. (ii)

Δ

```
              asstralylogism
          bemesticatorialloodge
       ismaticsologismahybrodomina
  undamentalis                ment
ipplestimule                  iy
hypenaltern                   tl
    soolipsis                 j
    aglasm
     armag
      ure
      rimp
        ape
          ma
           tle
            min
              tle
              it
              em
                ll
```

                    hollowgram
            isoment   iderheate
        ollegirmoil   irthday
          clipsme   eople
      eyephaun   drea
    idolitra   ored
                                askker
                    ime   ibissit
                                nkt
                            own
                            aver
                          shi
                      myopis
                    limbus
                    goest
                    wes
                  taer
              tes
          sew

                        slesh off
              cloose no   aased pow
          shes   slisp
      nop   oon
      lip
      l
      i
      sply
        esh
          aste
            lungg
                numenuseum
              harmon
          car
          ril
          ade
      spil
          sampl
                reenwet
                    asp

aglissiphypno
ifret   addwichmass
milkso   plastotrngluw
ison   instammar
st   arrata
i   mist
l   sli
o   clo
t   ea
i   si
j   drem
               cun
               ts
               e
               id
               ol
               si
               ul
               pe
               sn
               is
               so
               if
               i

                    nli
                    sh
                   istle
                 usculari
              decresscenation
          profal   staasis
        hypnot   chrodo
      gastrop   rhythm
        wer   atu
       myg   cide
      ott   ther
     embr   reea
     somb   ond
    shiu   ic
   golo   sa
   spi   ef
   pi   hi
   &   bel
    t   isma
                       illo
                      smoa
                       drast
                       folor
                      exual
                       itsnic
                        endoshi
                       gallis
                        frem
                        ast
                        ga
                        sm
                        ill
                        dra
                        th
                         l
                          o
                           i

```
          nessage
   emr        ticcle
 ebr            irless
 ilic            icas
  isp           oon
   il           fo
    i          piss
    to      ali
     ing ma
      sow
       old
      ost
     et
   alll
  in
   roe
   oth
     rill
      mi
        rro
       ls
         y
```

if
uh
snuf
cunup
rhyththm
darkark
less
oon
li
t

```
              h
              o
             mu
            oodli
             ih
             li
              n
             im
              tti
            nuu
           ehaolgg
            aalastiv
                istubula
                onoclasm
                mgmai
          gular    sall
         unumb     dbi
         odb       hy
       numeno      il
       mmilio      u
       nhilis      t
         mi
         uck
          ggag
          es
          li
         mo
         nep
         i
         ily
          o
          j
```

canoptic
mistasikudra
fecundatioaterb
iranyongl   iulm
azepe   liib
oll   ei
in   uy
ili   iu
oy   o
ei   li
uh   ni
ai   im
un   pi
ig   icj
y   al
             ul
             is
             yi
             e
             a
             ii
             j

th
eb
ar
or
we
fo
se
ea
an
db
ar
th
eb
ar
or
we
fo
rs
ea
an
db
ar

The Primary Universe is fraught with great peril. War, plague, famine and natural disaster are common. The Fourth Dimension of Time is a stable construct, though it is not impenetrable. Incidents when the fabric of the fourth dimension becomes corrupted are rare. If ghost machines occur, they will be highly unstable. Ghost machines are able to contact the Living Receiver through the Fourth Dimensional Construct. No one knows how or why the Living Receiver is chosen. When the Living Receiver awakens, they are often haunted by the experience. Many of them will not remember. (iii)

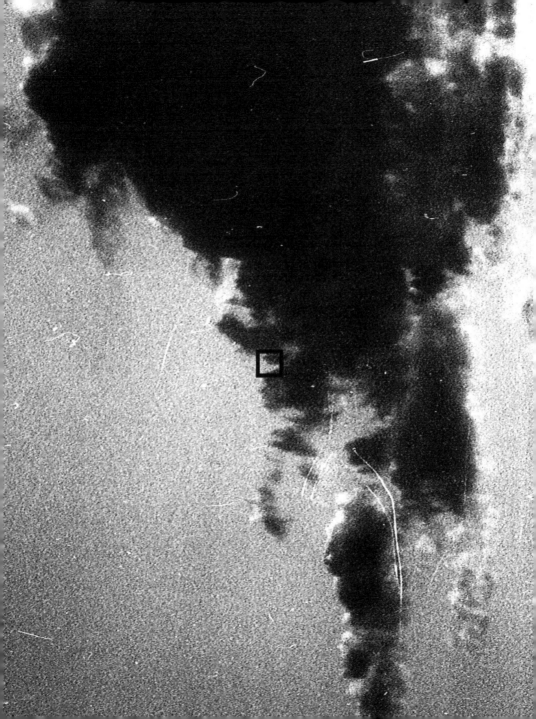

static continues

in the evening on white paper

shadows and ice

filling the void

echoes pierce the light

Missile Command until 3:00 AM

all flash no substance

motes of dark are functioning

the stolen Eyes of friends

echo in the dark

in the evening on white paper

drinking orange soda reading the news

the world is ice

shadows and ice

filling the void

a frozen lung tree

pulses its swimming bells

in the evening on white paper

static continues

filling the void

in the evening on white paper
motes of dark are functioning
echoes pierce the light
the world is ice
shadows and ice
preparing for an entrance
Dear Hibernation:
motes of dark are functioning
capsules of the night
wet with dew

protect your cities

from falling warheads

in the evening on white paper

the world is ice

echoes pierce the light

capsules of the night

wet with dew

preparing for an entrance

static continues

filling the void

Dear Annihilation:

no Eye am not going to be destroyed

floating in the dark

wet with dew

wires dance in the wind of the noise

the stolen Eyes of friends

filling the void

the world is ice

shadows and ice

echoes pierce the light

behind its screen the soul is quiet

capsules of the night

protect your cities from falling warheads

in the evening on white paper

the world is ice

echoes pierce the light

shadows and ice

wet with dew

preparing for an entrance

static continues

in the domain of eternal night

3 cups 2 donuts

floating in the dark

the stolen Eyes of friends

wet with dew

in the evening on white paper

protect your cities from falling warheads

filling the void

Dear Annihilation:

no Eye am not going to be destroyed

in the evening on white paper
a frozen lung tree
filling the void
Missile Command until 3:00 AM
falling warheads
wet with dew
wires dance in the wind of the noise
echoes pierce the light
in the domain of eternal night
buttermilk pancakes $4.95

static continues
the stolen eyes of friends
filling the void
fading in the dark
empties half-empties roaches
Space Invaders until 3:00 AM
static continues
in the domain of eternal night
preparing for an entrance
wet with dew

preparing for an entrance
in the evening on white paper
Eye write about static
falling warheads
wet with dew
filling the void
figment in the dark
echoes pierce the light
preparing for an entrance
all flash no substance

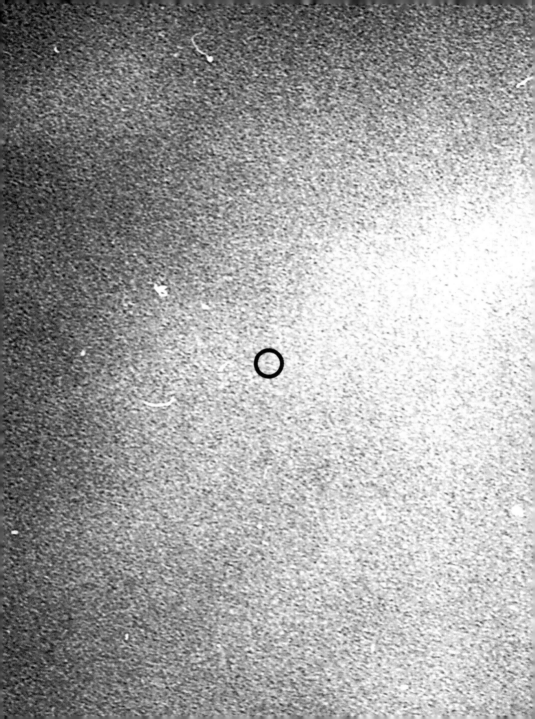

The title of this book would justify the inclusion of Prince Hamlet, of the point, of the line, of the surface, of n-dimensional hyperplanes and hypervolumes, of all generic terms, and perhaps of each one of us and of the godhead. In brief, the sum of all things—the universe. We have limited ourselves, however, to what is immediately suggested by the words 'ghost machines'; we have compiled a handbook of ghost machines conceived through time and space. We are ignorant of the meaning of the ghost machines in the same way that we are ignorant of the meaning of the universe, but there is something in them that fits our imagination, and this accounts for their appearances in different places and periods. (iv)

X

ren dter

corp soem

ift swem

biolim ess

voi dling

ong ular

fap p

rif ( ) tird

laung ( ) ole

numi ( ) naut

meye ( ) tilts

exil ( ) eng

```
        /\
    / thin\gk \
    \ teye/ime /
    | ide\ads |
      \ lo/s /
        \ts/
         \/
```

\\ s

ea \\

ment \\

// knofake \\

//ashlangaggin \\

\\ blacortex //

//erebelum //

\\ zone //

\\ gla

s\\

*

* or *

* if *

* ice *

*

(i)

(iso)

(isle)

(it)

(r)

(ip)

(werk)

(un)

(d)

(i)

(reamd)

(eyem)

(e)

{

{}

{o}{}

{m}{}

{}

{}

{}{un}

{}{mare}

{}{org}

{}{on}

{}

{if}{}

{t}{}

{}

{}

{}{im}

{}{e}

{}

{

:::::::: hy :::::::::::

:::::::::::: pn ::::::::::::::::::::::

::::::::::: autic ::::::::::::::::::::::::

:::::::: langulat :::::::::::: ion :::::::::::

::::::::::: unlight::::::::::::::::::::::::

:::::::::: occularitus ::::::::::::::::::::::::

::::::::::::::::: icthivoids ::::::::::::::::::::

::::::::::: orgotlens ::::::::::::::::::

:::::::::::::::::::::::::: faice ::::::::::::::::::

::::::::::::::::: shado :::::::::::::

::::::::::: we :::::::

:::::::: ill :::::

{}

atmostear

{} aginalia

un {} lackbox

cye {} sumone

{} nightall {}

scarfice {}

exo {} unlit

{} induh

arkless {}

{}

lotu [] scular

[] dimbryo [] gogic

[] ormsky []

shilts [] smere []

eyerot []

ghost machines are empty jewels / figment plays a filtering role / the spectrum of ambient light / dots the abyssal night / death is the first wavelength to be absorbed / surprising and disorienting the machine / anyone who has seen a ghost machine will keep an image of it / in their memory forever / for its isolation, for its cosmic cold, its eternal obscurity / adapted for collecting the maximum available night / with no teeth, no poison, and no shell / soft bodied machine with no strings / an almost complete transparency / fills its cavity with ink (v)

static in the dark
a frozen lung tree
pulses its swimming bells
the stolen Eyes of friends
crawling on figment
small thin tubes
to drink things dissolved and diluted
a knife in a star is just as much
static is canceled
just as much

darkling nodes pick up words

small thin tubes

to drink things dissolved and diluted

the fingers and the teeth

floating in the dark

the weakest part

floating in the dark

figment in the ark

a frozen lung tree

fills its cavity with ink

sound machine

filling the void

a tune of non-being

fi((ing the void

the shadows and the teeth

the stolen Eyes of friends

***)ill! the void

a knife in a star is just as much

f&##}} the void

just as much

a tune of non-being

+=[][]ing the void

and sound machine

!!//::g the void

a tune of non-being

(%%%%%) the void

below 6000 m. depth

the stolen Eyes of friends

87&&$>> the void

a tune of non-being

darkling nodes

dot the abyssal night

fragments in the dark

▯▯▯▯▯ the void

a knife in a star is just as much

static is canceled

just as much

a frozen lung tree

pulses its swimming bells

fills its cavity with ink

in the domain of eternal night

an almost complete transparency

pulses its swimming bells

fills its cavity with ink

echoes pierce the light

the stolen Eyes of friends

(-_-) the void

no Eye am not going to be destroyed

in the domain of eternal night

wet with dew

and sound machine
| | | | | | | the void
pulses its swimming bells
below 6000 m. depth
small thin tubes
the fluid in the channels runs black
a tune of non-being
eating tiny capsules of the night
to generate sound
))))))) the void

and sound machine

echoes in the dark

wet with dew

below 6000 m. depth

and sound machine

echo in the ark

wet with dew

an almost complete transparency

pulses it's swimming bells

fills its cavity with ink

and sound machine
a frozen lung tree
pulses its swimming bells
in the domain of eternal night
below 6000 m. depth
a knife in a star is just as much
a tune of non-being
just as much
static is canceled
just as much

a tune of non-being

tends to get separated

+[0] [0]+ the void

a knife in a star

tends to get separated

<) 0 () 0 (> the void

sound machine

tends to get separated

f () ll () ng the void

no Eye am not going to be destroyed

a frozen lung tree
pulses its swimming bells
the stolen Eyes of friends
dot the abyssal night
motes of dark are functioning
small thin tubes
to drink things dissolved and diluted
a knife in a star is just as much
static is canceled
just as much

and sound machine
a frozen lung tree
pulses its swimming bells
fills its cavity with ink
in the domain of eternal night
below 6000 m. depth
a knife in a star is just as much
a tune of non-being
just as much
static is canceled

And if Eye understand the ghost machines, why can't Eye explain them? Knowledge, the ghost machines believe, resides only in particulars. Eye try to tell them that all words are plastic. Word images begin to distort in the instant of utterance. Ideas imbedded in a language require that particular language for expression. This is the very essence of the meaning within the ghost machines. See how it begins to distort? It is an outside frame of reference, a particular system. Dangers lurk in all systems. Systems incorporate the unexamined beliefs of their creators. Adopt a system, accept its beliefs, and you help strengthen the resistance to change. Does it serve any purpose for me to tell the ghost machines that there are no languages for some things? (vi)

motes of {:@:}
are functioning

capsules of
the night

echoes pierce
the light

shaped
like sleep

wet with dew

[(ii) Bontecou, Lee. *Lee Bontecou: A Retrospective*. Chicago Museum of Contemporary Art, 2008 / (iv) Borges, Jorge Luis, *The Book of Imaginary Beings*. Penguin. 1967 / (vi) Emperor Leto, "The Stolen Journals," *God Emperor of Dune*, 1981 / Hecker, Tim, "Where Shadows Make Shadows," *An Imaginary Country*. Kranky, 2009 / Rilke, Rainer Maria. "No I'm Not Going to Be Destroyed..." *The Unknown Rilke*. Oberlin College Press, 1990 / (iii) Sparrow, Roberta. "The Philosophy of Time Travel." *Donnie Darko*, 2001 / Spicer, Jack. "A Text Book of Poetry." 1960-61. / (i) Unknown, *Heroes of Might & Magic V*. Ubisoft, May 24th, 2006 /(v) Various (Albert I of Monaco. Beebe, William. Monod, Theodore.) *The Deep: Extraordinary Creatures of the Abyss*. University of Chicago Press, 2007.]